Under Sleep's New Moon

Other Books by Joseph Hutchison

Poetry
Eyes of the Cuervo/Ojos del Crow
The Satire Lounge
The World As Is: New & Selected Poems, 1972–2015
Marked Men
The Earth-Boat
Thread of the Real
Sentences
Greatest Hits: 1970–2000
The Rain at Midnight
The Heart Inside the Heart
Bed of Coals
House of Mirrors
Sweet Nothing Noise
The Undersides of Leaves
Thirst
Shadow-Light
Weathers, Vistas, Houses, Dust

Translation
Ephemeral (from the Spanish of Miguel Lupián)

Editor
Legions of the Sun: Poems of the Great War
Malala: Poems for Malala Yousafzai (with Andrea Watson)
A Song for Occupations: Poems About the American Way of Work
(with Gary Schroeder)

Under Sleep's New Moon

Rescued Poems, 1970–1990

Joseph Hutchison

The New York Quarterly Foundation, Inc.
Beacon, New York

NYQ Books™ is an imprint of The New York Quarterly Foundation, Inc.

The New York Quarterly Foundation, Inc.
P. O. Box 470
Beacon, NY 12508

www.nyq.org

First Edition

Set in New Baskerville

Layout by Raymond P. Hammond

Cover Design by Raymond P. Hammond

Cover Art: "Skeltz 1: Heart" by John Ransom

Library of Congress Control Number: 2021935193

ISBN: 978-1-63045-074-8

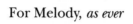

For Melody, *as ever*

ACKNOWLEDGMENTS

I wish to thank the editors of the following publications for choosing the following poems, some in very different versions:

Abraxas: "The Crow-Man"
The Adirondack Review: "Origins" and "Mountains
    from a Window at Terrebonne Elementary"
Last Stanza Poetry Journal: "Goodbye Kiss," "The
    Hands in Sleep," and "Valley Morning"
Mad Blood: "The Brain"
Naugatuck River Review: "Purple Heart"
New: Canadian and American Poetry: "Seventeen"
    (as "Poem from My Seventeenth Year")
New Salt Creek Reader: "A Ritual"
Open: Journal of Arts & Letters: "Black Willow"
Poet and Critic: "The Branch" (as "Fly He Said"—This
    poem appears in its original form in my
    new and selected poems, *The World As Is.*)
Poetry Australia: "Winter Owl"
Santa Fe Literary Review: "Desert Kingdom"
Sight Unseen: "Kai" (as "An Animal Death")
Verse Virtual: "Storm Over the Flatirons,"
    "Rockhound" (as "Fossil Hunter"),
    "Illumination at Midnight"

CONTENTS

—— The Left Side of Time ——

— A Cry of Desire —

— Lexicomania —

— The Genius of Trees —

Under Sleep's New Moon

Author's Note

A poet who tries to rescue an early poem is like a lifeguard who's dragged a moribund swimmer out of the surf. The job is simply to coax the wretch back to life: no pushing to make it join one's political party, no trying to inspire its conversion to one's latest religion. Enough to help it cough up some cloudy water and successfully catch its breath; enough to bring some color back into the poem's cheeks, and woo a bit of light back into its eyes, and help it sway to its feet—then send it on its way without passing judgment on its figure or fitness for society. Society after all must be a bit disorienting for the poem, which was born far away and in a different age. For the poet, the poem will always have a whiff of the stranger about it, even as its recovery affirms the choice not to let the ocean gobble it down. There is always the possibility, of course, that the poet's heroism is merely egotism wearing a shiny silver whistle. For the reader's sake, this poet hopes it isn't so.

I would have all know that when all falls
In ruin, poetry calls out in joy....

—W. B. Yeats,
"The King's Threshold"

Once the truth was ready ... it didn't care how it came.

—William Stafford,
"The Rescued Year"

And the brain kept blossoming
all through the body, until the bones themselves could think,
and the genitals sent out wave after wave of holy desire....

—Galway Kinnell,
"The Call Across the Valley of Not-Knowing"

A Kind of Radiance

Headwaters

Snowmelt trickles,
               spills
from the tundra moss
to bracken,
           growing
gabby, lusty—then
lapsing into reedy
ground,
only to pour itself
down channels farther on.

Toward sleep years later
I sometimes hear
that rush—
           confiding
blather at the inner ear.
Only my dreams
make clear
           what it says,
and the more I ache
to waken its gist,
the more the water's
sly essay
         slurs
toward ocean noise....

So I sleep to follow
the stream's cold story
as it feels its way
blindly
        over one
certain rock, its long
fingers reading
             into light
the face that dreams
so deep and secret there.

Damming the Creek

in our fifteen-year-old
prime
    we heaped
stream-slick stones,
     tried
  to dam the creek—
  laughing,
     grunting, bare feet
gripping into a slippery
wash of pebbles,
           or a mush
  of sand,
    faces flushed
as we labored, stacking
     stone
     on
     stone

*

the creek poured nevertheless
over and through it—so that
  when we walked back
  to camp toward sundown,
    rolled jeans soaked,
    feet fish-belly white
    and cold,
  your father shook his head,
sipped whiskey
       and, on the iron
   spit he'd brought from home,
turned the three fish he'd caught
over the fire he'd built alone

*

later   in our dark tent
we listened to the spring creek
mimicking
            moon-driven sea, rushing
    over boulders, sodden logs,
    beer cans,
            carrying
    watery handfuls of fine-washed silt
    toward the far
            Pacific—
and through the tent's
breathing window screen
we could see, glittering out
from a luminous cavern of cloud
above the massive black
silhouette of the Indian Peaks,

    O   R   I   O   N

who we did not know would come
again and again to guide us

Seventeen

Sunlight
on a pond, blurred
ripples reflected on the ceiling
above the drawn curtains.

The room otherwise
dark. His bones leak a blue
inkish liquid ... it
fills the room, floats before him
in little pulsing globules.
He's adrift in zero gravity....

In the kitchen,
mother speaks in a low voice to his father.
She wonders what the boy is
doing in there on a fine
July afternoon—he is
seventeen and she suspects, she
suspects....

Father must be nodding his head,
touching big fingers to the back
of her hand that trembles
as she worries an invisible nub
between her forefinger and thumb
like a grain of truth....

The boy doesn't care.
Red ants swarm
out of his nostrils ...
bees drip from his armpits
thickly ... until his bones
are dry and hollow—
they'll creak if he moves....

Now he finds himself
studying the shadows curled up
where the baseboards have cornered them,
and his gaze gathers them
in, hears them breathe. He leans
toward what is his, toward
the living darkness under the bright
surface of the shuddering water
outside in the world.

Midnight at Grand Lake

July's full moon
           lacquers the lake's hectic
                                  ripples

                              black
             absence races toward me
between the lines

A Kind of Radiance

The Lower Falls

The Yellowstone River rolls
like some sleeper in slow
motion tumbling

out of bed. Over
the canyon's lip, it
freefalls, plunges

into the mist that ghosts
up from the granite basin
invisible to see. A cold-

clawed vertigo climbs
the spine, its reptilian
tail tightens around

the cervical bones, its
thin hands digging to grip
the brain's almondish knots

until their panic
flares—a black light
that is a kind of radiance.

Hanging Lake

This lake is blue as the secret
light in a saint's eyes.
Snow-fed, fishless, and at bottom
a jumble of mossy branches.
Even a clear life,
says the pond, is cluttered.
But the wind that gusts over it,
blurring the depths, says:
Nothing is wholly true
whose clarity is only calm.

Storm Over the Flatirons

Rain veils trailed
by slate gray clouds
brush the shadowed peaks

as if some forgotten
grief in the body brawled
out into the shaken air

thick drops strike
the massive granite
outcrops now

cold white
flashes
in the dark billows

send ripples of thunder
shuddering
under

the climber's skin

Ancient Light

in a dog's eyes the ancient
light appears and beneath it
the prairie lopes and rolls
and yips of joy startle
jackrabbit and chipmunk
meadowlark and blackbird
into scrambling flight

in a dog's eyes
the ancient light is a tall
body the winds
swirl through like water
in a water clock
making the bluestem grass
bend under the weight
of passing time

in a dog's eyes the ancient light
gleams in the prairie's veins
those winding streams
that summon to their clarities
the small birds that sip
and sing singing
wakefulness into the world

A Strong Branch

No friends tonight. No
lover. Tree crickets
that *chirr-chirr-chirred* all week
are silent now. I wander this
empty Denver street

and there is only
the rush of my breathing,
as if a black-capped
night heron were
falling through me toward

a strong branch,
knowing it is there, knowing it
is
down there, in
the dark.

Drought

Sky swollen again, the dark
Olympian garments glimpsed
from where we crouch, dry
hands held out. We are slaves
to this false season; there's thunder
of feasting ... but scant drops
fall. We have sent up men
with offerings of silvery ice,
and still They are indifferent.
We knew Their names once, knew
how to summon Them. We have
walked hip-deep in deity.
It was long ago.

Rockhound

       July sun makes the windless
air tremble   no birds
and the grass still
as if rooted in the floor
of an invisible lake

  I walk rubbled hills
where rocks I hammer open
lay bare
          imprinted ferns
          trilobites
          shell traces

  and sweat creeps down
over my ribs:
   body
         remembering sea

Desert Kingdom
(after the photograph by Steven Hays)

Bisti Wilderness, New Mexico

What are these battered beasts
from a time before words? Heaved

up out of the desert's bleached
grit, they point blunted faces

into a wind the camera's put
a stop to. Locked in place, how

can they be so moving? It must be
some creature inside us recalls

these familial shapes. We feel its
head lift in dim recognition, feel it

groan under the thundering flood,
this sun-struck river of clouds.

A Crumpled Map

Origins

Infants reaching out
with one hand
cling
with the other.

The births and deaths
of nations
begin
with this division.

Button

When her toddling
firstborn tumbled
hard to the sidewalk,

her eyes blurred
like a misted
kitchen window when

something nourishing's
boiling on the stove.
The boy's teeth-

gritted, tear-mastering
grimace made her
touch, unthinkingly,

the blouse bodice pulled
askew by her indrawn
breath, touch

the smooth
pearl button sewn
loosely above her heart.

Rough Fruit

It was a scraggly raspberry hedge, and it ran the length of the backyard fence, one of those four-foot wire fences common in those years when America felt safe because it had rescued the world. The intimacy of that thicket, the solitude ... the ragged, midsummer leafiness of its voice ... the tunnels I'd crawl into getting out of the heat, all hung with lamps like Christmas lights—some the flushed color of pomegranates, others richer like drops of red wine. Whole afternoons I'd lie in those hallways with their low ceilings and walls woven of scratchy branches. Flat on my back with a cheek-full of seedy berries, I'd doze and sway toward a shadowy depth like a bucket swung in over the stone lip of a well. Breezes hissed through chinks in the leafage, scattering a confetti of sunlight over my carefree face and my white, size ten tee-shirt streaked with juicy intensities. I'd pretend not to hear my mother calling me in for lunch, and instead snuggled farther in, and pinched more prickly sweet-tartnesses off their twigs, and mashed them against the roof of my mouth....

Gone now, that careless seclusion ... lost in this America of stranger-friends and tweet storms, drone cameras, hungry "cookies" ... or possible only when eating raspberries—crushing them, tonguing the tiny seeds from between my teeth, feeling the rough fruit light up the dark, watery cloister of my mouth....

Fallen Branch

A cottonwood branch, sheared
off by lightning, gropes up
out of the weeds. From a three-walled
treehouse twenty feet up, the boy
leans to look down at it.

Still August air.

Far off, clouds
sail high over massive
peaks. The boy feels
the tree curving away beneath him.
And when his eye catches
sight of something
dark—a tremor among the burdocks—
the fallen branch shudders
and the treehouse
sways....

By the time he's scrambled
to the ground, breathless,
the boy has chosen (unknowingly)
his path: a brick house
in the 'burbs, job in the city,
the lightning bolt deep
in his chest at sixty.

The clouds passing over
seem to whisper, "Patience..."
but the boy has already mounted
his bike and, bent
low over the handle bars,
hears nothing but the zip of gears,
the hiss of his tires
on the asphalt turned sticky
by the merciless sun of summer.

A Conqueror's Ship

Across a snowy moonwashed field one night my childhood came sailing like a movie theater. Ripe with odors of popcorn and licorice and Hershey bar wrappers it came gliding, and I saw it was a galleon heavy with a cargo of children. In the hold, the children cheered as they peered up through the hatches thrown open under a dizzying star field, though the stars were merely painted on the night ceiling. The children huddled in rows, and all faced a screen that loomed like a vast mainsail, where they watched white heroes blast dusky villains from lathered horses, or outfox Red nations by trading vast grasslands for cat's-eye marbles and whiskey, or make vampires rot rapidly away by casting upon them the shadows of crosses....

Up front, a glassed-in cashier read and re-read the same page of a crack-spined novel again and again with no trace of enjoyment. And no tickets were sold. No tickets were ever sold because the children had been born to that darkness, born to cheer at each climactic scene, though all the movies had played a thousand times, and the children knew each word and gesture by heart. Why the ticket booth with its bored cashier existed is one of the mysteries, along with the exit doors that weren't doors at all but images painted on the black walls.

Through a snowbound field my early life coasted past like a conqueror's ship. It carried treasures I had no name for—treasures for kings I didn't know existed! And as if from a great distance I could hear us all laughing or gasping in the hold, now whooping in unison, now breaking into song ... while the chains of happiness were ringing....

A Rose for Charlie

I have seen the red rose burning
and this means more.

      —Charles Bukowski (1969)

the rose burning
vermilion deep
with a sweet
pink flush
where the sepals
unfurl their greens

yes of course
beautiful

but a Buddhist
in Vietnam
burning
in the street?
granted that act
is ugly, the charcoaled
peaceable corpse
toppling
in the end
but

why did you claim
the rose means more?

a man burns
and we sit back (noses
plugged
in cool petals)
and judge?

well, Charlie, not
this kid

Purple Heart

Fort Logan National Cemetery, 1970

Mowing the government's grass
for college cash, I happen
on your name—
                    a shock
            to see they've tied it
    and the gentleness it signified
to a white slab (like weighing
    down a sack
                    of kittens)—
yet it floats
                up to me now through
gone years
                and tree-shadowed soil

                    you died
"in action"
one year out of high school
and my grief is
                    that remote

I remember so little about you

    my heart feels swaddled
in old newspapers

I turn away, look up:

across the "memorial walkway"
    big machines
                like yellow
                scorpions still
                sting
                    the Earth

digging the government's graves...

41

Vietnamization

Northwest Denver, 1981

They shoulder sticks with bags
tied on like brown cocoons
on branches. At all the fences,

dogs go wild, but having heard dogs
at their backs before—and worse—
the Asians ignore them. You

guess they're husband and wife,
and often wish their curious eyes
might find this window, your

sympathetic face. But each day
they dart intently from bin to bin,
digging up and sacking your discarded

goods. Somewhere, the trash transforms
into wings of crisp American cash—
a kind of victory. And for that

you admire them. You admire them
as your dog bounds along the fence,
barking the refugees on down the alley.

Peasant Heart

History is a nightmare from which
I am trying to awake.

—James Joyce

Being suddenly empty and aloof, your mind
watches history wheel—nightmare of crimes
turning up over and over like sour scraps
of a drunkard's dinner. But such bitter
images flummox the heart, bump
up against the mind's obsessive sleepwalk
inside your aching psyche; failed notions
slip out through some hole in your convictions—
and bending to retrieve them, a table-corner barks
its simple quiddity into your skull, the whole
house spinning as galaxies scatter....

                              Then,
as in the beginning, your peasant heart
takes over. New prospects appear. The heart's
swaying hay cart creaks over a hill toward morning.

A Stalk of "Aaron's Rod"

Alone on the hillside, a dry
stalk of dead mullein twitches
in the wind that combs the long

tawny grass. With each gust
the grass so flexibly defers to,
the stiff mullein stalk whips
from side to side or draws

cramped circles on the sky;
and when the rippling grasses
suddenly lapse back, the parched
mullein stills too, but stands

erect as some grim evangelist,
head thrust rigidly upward,
emptied of every last thought.

The Brain

can be a fist thrust up
by the spine; it can knot
like a testicle, unfold
like a rose, turn black
(a stone in the gut
of a glacier). Because
the brain is silent,
like heaven, we forget
that, whatever we call it,
it's also a crumpled map
of the infinite: day after day
we throw it away.

The Left Side of Time

Kai

Collar twisted tight, her white
body like an eyeless statue
hung from the gate she'd tried
to climb, and the wind in my chest
stalled. With trembling hands, I
brushed flies from her crumpled ears,
hugged her, lifted her, untwisted
her collar from the gate-top scroll,
and laid her, lean and rigid,
down on the lawn her straining paws
had nearly reached. Seconds
prickled my skin like icy flakes
blasted sideways in a mean
high-country storm. I kneeled,
stroked her thin summer fur,
and felt a heartless weather
seething in it, a blizzard whirling
steadily down from the mountains,
terribly white.

A Distant Whistle

A last spasm shoved him
to one side of the bed
and his heart waved goodbye
as the train he had boarded
leaned into a curve

the invisible cars the silent engine
tang of lack in the barren room

and the nurse
glancing through the electric window
marked his bead of light
droning slow and level along the horizon

later as the body was dollied away
she felt the smooth floor tremble

one wheel
screeching its harsh dismay
like a distant whistle the wind
brings home to us

faintly
over the fields in winter

Blue Footprints

I
Out of their long seclusion, up
from the mud, from the bottoms

of rivers and lakes, the dead come
wearing bracelets of coarse snow,

wearing amulets of glassy ice.
Out of dusty arroyos and windy

canyons they come with tongues
of jagged chalcedony that clack

in their hollow mouths. Out
of oblivion they arise

with their pallor, with their
bleak silence, with their stares.

II
Out of oblivion they have come
sallow-faced, with their breath
of damp wood trying to burn,
their hands reeking of wet ashes.

Out of our own bodies they come
seeking something lost or long ago
left behind, something cool and green
with a fragrance of peeled logs....

III
They come most in the night,
approaching us from white winter
pastures, walking white roads.
In our bedrooms they come

close to us, bending down
to gaze into our faces, touching
our eyes and mouths with their stiff
fingers, until their tongues
grow still, and their stubborn silence
winds through us like faintly blue
footprints in January snow.

Faithless

again my death has touched me
a glove of ice

one day I'll wake
with it there   a chill
creeping up my left arm

now   my failures lay
heaped around me   each
still warm   each one's torn
skin leaking my lies

my eyes have no faith in my voice

my tongue   like a slug
stuck to a hot slab
of flagstone   stiffens
when I think to truly speak

how many lives have I
wasted this way   locked
in bodies with vacant names

believing there was time

The Left Side of Time

after Dalí

The mouth is a wound in the left side of time. The eyes, holes in its palms. So there is a Christ in each of us, a clock-weight that makes the heart pound. And every heartbeat tolls the hour of our—

Are we sleeping or awake? Or both at once? Or neither...

Listen: the mountain bleeds wind, invisibly—only a few pines ticking. The dreamers groan, cry out, struggle upright ... find the clock's red numerals branded on some prison wall....

Or say the dreamers dream on, clutching their pillows....

Either way, who'll release them?

Embraced by night. Stunned by the Earth's hungry kiss.

The Flowering

Another night with his fear
that the flowering in her
is ending. *Has* ended?
Only this blind longing
keeping him from seeing it?
Him, face buried in his pillow,
writhing, or suddenly sitting
up for breath. Feeling ashamed,
feeling lost. Then sleeping at last.
Going down into the earth of it.
Dissolving into roots. Rising
through them in the dark. Seeing
what the flower sees: the two
of them in the open window,
naked in moonlight, or at ease
on the mountain, or tearful
under leaves, in tangled grass.
Then flowering more. Bending
under the beauty of seeing
clearly, seeing whole. Bowing
in pain and in joy. Bearing
the difficult witness.

Goodbye Kiss

A kiss flares up from fear
or expectations of loss.
Don't leave, it pleads,
already in mourning as

the farewell descends
like a bell jar....
The avid kiss wavers,
the heart withdraws. Soon

there'll be nothing but words
like sparks blown from an ember,
flickering in a wire that stretches
from a number to a number.

Black Willow

Last night his heart
arched and gaped
like a fish flexing in
the rough grassy bed
of a creel. He kept

picturing them, bodies
fused, pleasing each other
as he lay suffering. Soon
he climbed out of bed,
stepped to the open window

and pressed his face
against the dusty screen
to breathe. He could hear
a river-rush of wind
shouldering clouds out

over the plains—but here,
dead stillness. Leaves
in the grove along the ditch
nearby, hung as if stunned.
Suddenly, just beyond

the grove, the clouds
parted, and a bright
crescent moon appeared,
caught up in the black
network of branches.

A Ritual

"I don't need dreams, Doctor...."
                    —Philip Roth

One eye drifts
beside the other,
wine barrels rolling
on waves. Alone,

a man gets drunk
on his body, hating
it, letting it happen.
The giddy bedroom

breathes him,
lavender of sweat
in the sheets.
Drowned

in her memory,
her body of air
and desire, even
his hands are

ashamed, sullenly
pumping the soured
milk. Stupid, this
blind ritual. Yet

he performs it:
making the god's
eyes burn in their
hogshead of blood.

Night Wind

Windowpanes shudder
in their shaken frames.
On the deck, the wrought

iron chairs stumble-dance,
their skeletal heels scraping
the splintery wood. A long

groan saturates the walls,
and something blindly
thumps the roof, the way

our savage heart thumps
under the ribs. Knowing
the ways of wind's no help

against what bristles now
in the labyrinth of the gut,
what makes the archaic knot

tied to the topmost spine-bone
fray and loosen. The house,
something tells us, can't hold;

what sweeps the sky tonight,
it says, will someday sweep
the ruined world away.

Insomnia

Morning all night in the chest

dawn of bloody clouds
rising past the ribs
of poplars

isn't it breath
this wind

so warm a wind

such a long sleep or landscape
isn't it

prairie wind
lifting a reluctant eyelid
lifting a leaf

or the moon a wave
in the breathing shell
of the chest

in this mournful
bloody twilight of the chest

The Water's Secret

I'm learning to live with the secret of silent water,
water that lies on its back in the well, mulling the darkness,
its surface blind to the clouds flowing over, the cherry blossoms
swaying like galaxies over the well's stone mouth, and the face
of the girl who peers down, looking for her lost golden ball.

I accept the moss that thickens like mucous in a sore throat,
and I accept the chill of the granite walls, and the hanging
bucket's rotted bottom, and the fraying rope that groans
faintly as its grip on the warped crank axle weakens.

If only fresh water would flood up into the well...
If someone would craft a new bucket, weave a new rope...
If the girl would undo her braids and shake out her golden hair...

But the story is strong: how darkness loves its silent water,
the water that holds it so completely in its arms ... water
that knows the clouds are too thin, the cherries won't come,
and the golden ball is gone into the heart of the Earth forever.

So the water lies back, thinking, thinking ... telling itself
this darkness isn't so bitter. *Other waters are far more bitter,*
it tells itself. *Look at the sea! My darkness isn't nearly as bitter
as the bitterness of the sea. No—my darkness is almost sweet.*

This is the secret I've learned I must learn to live with:
the endless entanglement of the bitter and the sweet.

A Cry of Desire

Flag Iris

... bulbs golden in the earth ...
—Odysseus Elytis,
"Axion Esti"

The eye in the back of the head
is like a bulb of flag iris, a cry

of desire in the Earth's grip.
Rooted in night, it shoots long

leaves and smooth stalks upward
into the light, where it unfurls

one of its nation's flags: white
of sea froth, bold yellow of suns

in children's paintings, pale blues
of the heavens inside a sapphire,

purple of bruises, purple of kings.
We are each free to refuse the hints,

choose another color or none at all.
But that golden bulb can't flaunt

colors other than its own, and we
can't un-see what it gives us to see,

the eye in the back of the head.

Escheresque

after "Relativity" (1953)

My desire is like a leafy birch
outside an arched window.
The frame shows only a tangle

of green, a nest, the broken
paper body of a child's
lost kite. But the spreading

roots are hidden, the crown
hidden. I must leave the house
to see the birch tree whole.

I'm scribbling this to prove
to myself I'm on the way,
racing through the stone house,

hunting for a door to the world
(I've forgotten where it is
though I built this place myself).

Am I closer than the last time
I dropped some crumbs of language
in the hall? Or is my trust in a door

nothing more than some distraction
for my longing as I wander
an endless labyrinth of stairs?

Bringer of Apples

Blue on the black
field her light the glow
of a hurricane
lamp through the mist

this is the dream
dreamt again night
after restless night

the basket
swinging the lantern
swinging its
brightness
kindling her hair
and her eyes the lamp
a fountain splashing
shadows her face
drowned

how long how many
years the flame
approaching
only approaching

I wake
the eyeless
fog at the glass
and again
the fragrance
of apples withering
on the air like
song

Spoken Under the Breath

The way at the edge
of seeing a certain brightness
hovers, your image
stays. But when I look quick—
is gone. My window opens

on scudding clouds, on roofs
like a wicked pack of cards
thrown down. What do you mean?
I'm lost—and I care—is all
I mean to say.

Somniloquy

"I slip off to the river,"
says the poet, "but she's
there in the shadows
a few chattering aspens
cast on the current. I run

on then, over ground
thick with tangled roots,
and in a clearing find
a stone circle with ashes
smoking in its chest,

but there she is, crimson
in the only live coal left.
Deeper into the wood then,
clambering, face turned
down to read the way,

the cuneiform of brown
pine needles, the trail
growing fainter as I go,
as I tire, and stumble,
collapse into a patch

of dry grass." The poet
sighs now, mutters, "How
vast this forest," sinking
back into fretful sleep
with his lips still moving.

The New Life

To escape the tyranny of objects,
he became the cry of an owl. Invisible
to the guards, he slipped like mist
through the barbed fences.

In the forest, he threw on a cloak
made from the blue fragrance
of spruce; against thirst, he drank
the cold of stones, the milk of stars.

Now the moon lies down beside him;
they talk of his new life. His voice
tries on color after color; his dreams
roll like shells in the gibberish of waves.

A Voice in the Dark

Say that words flare up from a dream. *Loquacious dusk,*
for example. A musical phrase. It allows the brain
a few seconds of complex electrical activity, giving rise
to a windchime shiver of feeling.
                        And coming steadily down as I
turn the words over—whether or not I turn them over—the dark
seems suddenly human; its voice, as implied by the phrase, arrives
laden with information both trivial and profound, its rhythm slow
but fluid, confidential, its register low enough to lull the listening self
as a child is lulled by adults who, thick with supper, talk weather, politics,
death. I pronounce the two words over and over just under my breath
until their sense is clear and my dullness fades. In fact, I feel
more awake than usual, alert in my body.
                        But fine perceptions
now scarcely matter, for the dark after all has come down
with its solitude, its speechless winds, its stars
in which we once read our lives, huddled by fires
that signaled far worlds when we slept.

Illumination at Midnight

Weary from wrestling a stubborn poem,
thoughts all thick red clay, he shuffles
sock-footed across the living room's
carpeted darkness, groping to find
the floor lamp's chain of beads. Now
his finger sparks, and the bulb drinks up
his body's charge, flares, winks out—
leaving this fading afterimage:

Adam sprawled on the Chapel sky,
drunk as a lord, his limp left hand
lifted toward the hand that made him;
but failing, failing ... he sinks back,
his listing head and cloudy gaze
lost beneath a cockeyed lampshade.

A Serious Gesture

Can it be your sighs
have hung the shaggy
morning grass with wet
diamonds? Let's be serious.
You're due for a serious gesture,

aren't you?
Maybe so; or
not. Go ahead:
doze awhile
longer. Who,

after all, cares if your mind
wanders? If you let that figure
in again ... the one you find
so disturbing, the one who holds
the long thorny stem of a rose

tight in his bloodied teeth.

The Sisters from a Window
at Terrebonne Elementary

Blown snow bright on a hard sky
like chalk-dust streaking slate.
Hulking up underneath, the three
peaks called The Sisters. What is it
they can school us in? The bitter

cold comfort that pines also groan,
their roots suffering, and dwindle
in number as they climb? That ascent
exhilarates but ends in solitude? Or
an even harsher truth: the heights

belong to nothing but wind.

The Crow-Man

The bicycle trundles past me on the roadside path, its rusty chain making mouse-like squeaks. The rider is an old man. He pedals slowly. He is careful not to let his black baggy pants get caught in the chain. His knees, as he pedals, lazily rise and each skinny leg in turn bends almost double....

How could I not have noticed?

His face is a crow's face! His sagging nose a beak. His way of bending forward in his black cloth coat is like a crow clutching a cedar branch in the wind. I pause to watch him pedaling away, dwindling into the distance.

Suddenly I can see him at nightfall, rolling along the gently curved breast of the piedmont. He steers down a deserted lane, presses his chest to the handlebars, and his legs stretch straight out behind him as he lifts into the air, the long black wings of his arms beating....

The bicycle clatters against a broken fence.

And he rises ... high over the sleepy farms, over cottonwoods and silvery threads of creeks ... his sleek feathers glossed by the light of the harvest moon.

Tonguefish

A mat of gulfweed lifts
on a midnight swell,
then slews down its sleek
midriff. Underneath,
Tonguefish

scatters his
silver intensities
like a skittery
star submerged
in the jet stream's

flood. He darts
and wriggles
through the moon's
mosaicked reflection
(its shards bright

as a Cubist cello's
hips), keen to nuzzle
the salt-rosined root
of its sway. Springing
up, arcing back

into the dithering wash,
Tonguefish nibblingly
feeds—savoring
the briny light at the core
of the world's desire.

Lexicomania

The Hands in Sleep

let go of your wrists
and crawl off into an ocean

therefore the vertigo
in your sudden
reach to kill the clock's alarm
the prickling in your fingers
like spirits called up
at a séance

therefore too
those skull-pounding
tidal rumblings as you wake
with your shaken sense
of having traveled deeply
through the dark

and touched
others of our kind

Panpipes

When the mournful mouths
opened in her wrists, their dark
voices clouded the hot bathwater.

Later that morning, the landlord
interrogated her tenant's lack.
"Who'll pay her back rent now?"

The young paramedic didn't know.

*

Weeks later she returned to class.
Smiles flickered around her,
neon bright, and no one spoke,
though her raw look said:
*These cheerful signals mean
you still don't see me...*

*

I'd agreed to read her poems aloud.
I was the teacher. It was my duty.

Like April clouds at dusk, the lines
were edged with a blood-orange light.

As I read, her nail-bitten fingers tapped
the stresses, trembling; then her hands,

like some shy orchestra conductor's,
began to move. I kept glimpsing

her wrists as the poems slipped
into my voice and away: it seemed

a vast pain were silently playing
the raw panpipes of her scars.

Undaunted

for Jim Doyle

We've gathered in this
windowless room to hear his words
the poems we are not sure
are his but someone else's maybe
someone famous

the sun's going down
over his shoulder but he
goes on undaunted
to get them out to get
them over
to us because

we have gathered here
after all to hear his true voice
hear the true words then go
home at last

and wonder whose life
he must be secretly living

Winter Owl

after The Carrier of Ladders

again his voice
sheds echoes
wings rushing low
over the Earth

and when at last
it rises a primal light
bathes my heart
my heart
that torques against
that mindful
grip

and now
the world below stops
becoming
reveals its essence
a radiant emptiness made
of whatever
given time
might happen

and I relax
into it
into this
moment of being
borne into the distance
of a dream
carried
out of time
toward a nest of snow

A Dusty Flame

Black lichen chafes
the young farmer's neck,
but he dozes anyway
against the rock
in the sun that kindles
windows in his lover's village;
her fingers slacken there
on the chair arm,
white and coolly curved
on the blue and green brocade.
They dream one dream:
red rays slanting at dusk,
wine-wet lips
in the shady garden,
the bee
like a dusty flame
in the folds of a rose.

The Other Life

after Robert Bly

I brush the other
life like the side of a barn,
a landlocked hull loaded
with hushed hens. My
fingers come back sore
with splinters, bristling
stubs of feathers. And death
stiffens inside me, hairs
all over my body stand
up. For a moment, my
heart and brain touch,
blind as raw yolks. They
sing to each other like two
snails mating under leaves
in Bolivia: the green wings
of seas glisten between them!

On a Photograph of Richard Yates

for Jill Krementz

Could I live enough to earn
a countenance like this?

Briary beard the color
of the curlew's tail;

eyes where light comes
to itself, startled

by heavy seas
below, shoreless

and bleak. Therefore
these age lines

tautened to stay
the tilting sail

of his voice—
that wide wing

kissing the deep
and turbulent waters.

A Short History of Existential Medicine

after Russell Edson

The corpse was having an enema.

Of course, this won't do any good, said
the doctor.

Why not? the corpse demanded.

My good man, you are already dead, explained
the doctor.

Isn't there a pill I could take for my condition?
cried the corpse.

Nothing would help, the doctor replied.

Then give me nothing! shrieked the corpse.

So the doctor gave him nothing.

Why not? thought the doctor with a shrug.
It couldn't hurt.

Lexicomania (and All that Jazz)

for Joe Nigg

We labor with language, our pointed wits
flashing like sewing needles in a sweatshop.
But it's no sweat. We like it. It keeps us
keen and intensely busy. Of course, it's
not the cloth—which fits or doesn't, lasts
or frays, flows out in patterns already dated
or slavishly in fashion—no, not the cloth,
but the cadence. A cadence that rocks us
around the clock like waves slapping a hull:
the tide we think in time with, though we know
its hubbub isn't the lilt of truths being woven,
but the unraveling palaver of our hearts.

Canonization

They made him a grave
inside of a yawn
made of his name a stone crow
and a book of its shadow

    then his silence
    was an underground river
    his voice a bare tree
    swayed by a dream

They made him a dream
inside of a stone
made of his name a grave voice
and a crow of its shadow

    then his book
    was a wind of yawns
    his silence a tree rooted
    near a dark river

They made him a river
inside of a dream
made his name a silent yawn
and a voice of its shadow

    then his grave
    was a tree made of stone
    his book a crow's nest
    rocked by the wind

Now he's a wind
    of underground dreams
his yawning grave
    a silence that makes
a crow of his voice
    of his name a green tree
and a book of his stone
    and a river of their shadows

The Genius of Trees

A Moment Just Before Dawn

Under wind-torn
clouds dyed indigo
by night, a dark flock
of starlings swerves,
loops and whirls,

weaving shining
threads of song
on the loom
of the willow's
leafless silhouette.

Maybe

When the long windy night begins
vanishing into the frozen earth,
our restless shadow returns to us
refreshed—like our mother's voice
that early one morning coaxed us
out of our cocoon of bedclothes,
calling us to watch the whitish frost
smoke as it let go of the rumpled grass
in the single-minded light of the sun.
Remember how our breath that day
surprised us, painting a glittery
ghost on the chilled window-glass?
We knew it would fade, but knew
also that any beauty our body made
might stay, maybe longer than *we* stay.
Even now that time has orphaned us,
wounded and healed us, we go on
sheltering in the sanctum of that *maybe*.

Equinox

The fall-fire of late sun's dyed
the pale green maple leaves—
clairvoyant orange, shades of red ...
histrionic as Vallejo's *I'll die in Paris*—
metaphor, until the future
makes it real.

*

In my sleep I've heard
some ghost jangling its chains
of events ... the links
ineluctable and random
as DNA. The point of death's
not circumstance—leaves
of the maple let go
when they must (though wind
has something of its way with them),
as we must let go when the ghost
insists....

*

Dusk ... and again the shape-
shifting body of the season works
against me ... moist waist
of mist, spine of frigid light—
I embrace you ...
like Mahler, half-celebrate
the chronic whiplash of vanishing....

Tiredness

It isn't enough to be tired of pain.
Pain must grow tired of you. But then

there's the tiredness: the way coals,

clinging to the thinnest flames, know
they've little left to feed them. How tired
we feel, watching fires falter while sleep

overwhelms us. No surprise. The dire

pantomime of any failing fire is far
too revealing to watch for long.

Mist

snags like a veil on the distant outcrops,
drops and folds into pines, into meadows;
nearer by, it creeps like spilled cream

in the just-dawn stillness ... deepening,
growing whiter the farther it flows.
It's the world as it was before the first

atmosphere decanted, before light honed
the edges of things and granted them
their tenacious realities. Maybe it's this

shifting translucence that throws you off
any time you try to interpret your grief:
shadowless mind in a world made of mist.

Instructive

This pencil in the water glass
I find instructive:

seeming bent, it is (when drawn
out) straight—arguing

the folly of sense, but hinting,
too, that a clearly unbent

object stood there
truly in the bending water.

Valley Morning

Snow crystals twinkling in morning wind,
mind alive to the light and that glacial peak

standing forth into it. Higher still, a cloud,
and a cloud, and a cloud. And the valley feels

full of ghosts: pale ones in yellow canvas pants,
or in checkered gingham and cobbled shoes,

darker ones in beaded deerskin moccasins,
in elk-hide dresses embroidered and fringed.

Like you, they all turned to this mountain,
and dreamed, and believed. Strange: how any

moment can deepen into years, even centuries;
how easily we can vanish into the images—

melting into time like a glint of snow....

Winter Music

No one among my neighbors saw
the clouds tear open over the mountains,
their fine net spilling
stars
  onto streets and houses, skittish
light clinging to branch and fence,
silk-weaving over the grass.
So that waking up

in the cold house, I rose
and looked out, amazed
as if I'd made it all happen
in my dream.
    And before sitting
down to breakfast, I let
joy drive me out

in coat, gloves and galoshes,
blue scarf and hat, to bend deep
into my own
    cloudy breath, wielding
a wide shovel. The rough walk's
hidden ache
    shivered up the hickory handle,
and the snow folded back like a wave
that spills out of
and into
   itself, or the flesh of a woman
baring the bones of her desire.
And as I worked

others joined me, men and women joined
their breath to my breath, the colors
of their scarves and their hats

and their namelessness
                    to mine, joined
their shovel-sound to the scrape
of my shovel,

till our labor was music
panting
           over the roofs of the day,
a sea of rough winter music that swelled
and spilled over
                    its time in the world,
that even now crests its silky
clarity through my life—
                    oceanic
spasm of awakening, cadence
of shoveling the walk.

Drifting to Sleep in the Orchard

for James Wright

New leaves calm overhead. But higher
up: a rumbling wind. The Pleiades
sparkle forth, then a dim gray
curtain of clouds is drawn
closed between us. Yet April

bends my spine like a green branch,
shadow-laden, starred with blossoms.
Their fragrance is a thread I long
to climb like braiding smoke
through a smoke-hole ... for if

a labyrinth hides inside me, so
must an exit.
                        Suddenly I realize
my body is some kind of boat,
a sailboat with a wind-tightened sail,
moving at ease under sleep's new moon.

Dreaming into Spring

That's why God made the movies.
                    —Paul Simon

As when the lovely-boned
woman on the bus
took me secretly into her mouth, I
know it's a dream. Buds
daring the air
like moans at a séance, the fine
rain of birdsong on the glass.
Hunched in time's
magic theatre, I watch
how the ambushed hero topples
to his feet, the bullets
screwing back
into the villain's gun. And why
try to wake up? It's good
to be here, amazed,
wanting to laugh, to come
alive. Slowly, I unwind
and breathe, feeling
the world reel its bitter tale
back to the sweet
sex scene.

A Clearing

His infamous talent
for bad timing—
what's become of it?
For they've come

together in perfect
rhythm, as others
sing in perfect pitch.
Whatever he feels, she

tells him, "It's okay."
Openness. Each breath
(for the first time
in his life, he tells her)

exactly as deep
as it needs to be.
As if he'd walked
out of a dark forest

into a clearing:
blossoms of cloud
in the wide sky;
blowing light;

time itself
at a standstill:
this long looking
into her eyes.

A Midsummer Night

Our moon strong through the hawthorn, brightness
streaming down, making even the shadows luminous.
The dark cry in me shakes like leaves at the thought
of your distant face as it drifts toward sleep....

Sweetness

A horse
broken through barbed wire
to cleave the alfalfa
drifts
like a low cloud now
whiskers of frayed
lightning
teeth bald as hammers
backbone gaunt
as an old man's longing
the eyes
huge
the eyes
shining dark as his memory
of rain one summer
when a storm
knocked down the pasture fence
and he wandered
into the orchard where limbs
hung low and thrashed
heavily in the leftover breeze
each branch weighed down
by countless small green apples
so tart when he nibbled them
that all the leaves
in the orchard
shivered
a moment as he moved
from tree to tree
searching for sweetness
among the boughs dripping
with dwindling
grumbles of thunder

The Genius of Trees

They hide their roots but flaunt
their branches: the topmost
twin and twine until the sky's
crazed and the eye's command's
bewildered. Fountaining slowly,
patiently, trees take years
to surprise the open fields, the hills,
the city-bound lawns. They let
leaves, needles, cones and catkins
fall with a flourish, reminding
the mind of its own shadow-thoughts,
the body of what it cannot name.
Knowing what they know
about birds and stones, about
how stirring wind can be,
they summon us as children
into their arms. And years
later, when they sway near us,
we feel carried off into the whirl
and tilt of the world, its days
and nights, its seasons—borne
up by the genius of trees.

CPSIA information can be obtained
at www.ICGtesting.com
Printed in the USA
BVHW031151110921
616359BV00002B/188